Flowering Meadows

Flowering Meadows

A BOUQUET OF POETRY
by
Paul Ray

Sonray Press
publisher

*Flowers are the sweetest things God ever made
and forgot to put a soul to.*
HENRY WARD BECKFORD
[1759-1844]

For information, contact:
Sonray Press, 1320 Cedar Lane, Charlotte, NC 28226

Printed In the United States of America
Sonray Press First Edition

Cover and layout format by gary hixson
ISBN 978-0-578-08188-5

Dedicated to
jane and gary
with love

Table of Contents

[TABLE OF CONTENTS]

[TABLE OF CONTENTS]

Preface

I've observed from watching my college-aged kids that they enjoy listening to music. Correction. That would be a slight understatement. I've observed from watching my college-aged kids that they enjoy listening to lots and lots of music. To be even more precise, they enjoy listening to rock, pop, rap, reggae, bluegrass and folk music which has been written and recorded within the past 40 years or so. It appears to be their favorite pastime. Morning, noon and night, my kids listen to music on their iPods and radios at home and everywhere they go. Their music will sometimes pour out loud and long into the evening, which, in the past, has brought about some parentally-set curfews.

Because of their great appreciation for and continual connection with music, both of my kids are phenomenal music aficionados. They are quick and accurate when it comes to naming the artist and the title of a song being played. Many times they even know all the lyrics and will actually sing along in key to the entire song while driving to school. It is an amazing thing to hear.

That being said, I have also observed something curious - they don't particularly like to read poetry at length, unless it is accompanied with a melody to which they can relate. I have seen this phenomenon with many other teens and college students, as well. When I asked them why they didn't like reading poetry, neither of them could give me a direct answer, even though they know that songs are just poems put to music. My daughter seemed to think that the words of a poem were not inspiring by themselves unless they were also accompanied by music. She said that her negative perception of poetry was hardwired in her brain because she could not easily draw meaning to the words unless there was some music joined with them to complete the thought.

My son, however, shared a different insight. It was his opinion that, if the words of a poem had a consistent tempo or beat, were accompanied with a simple and great moral message and were easy to understand, they had the potential of becoming both a great poem and a great song.

His definition of what might be considered great poetry could and should be debated. However, I believe his thought is a revelation on why poetry is not as popular today as it once was - music is seductive in that it carries one's mind along without the necessity of agreement with the lyrics. How many times have you sung along with a tune but weren't aware of what the words truly meant?

Poetry is much like a capella singing which has no music other than the words themselves. Some prefer musical accompaniment. This book, however, is written for those who enjoy the sound and meaning of words themselves as they express meaningful life experiences.

As the poet whose writings you have chosen today, I have strolled across many fields of my life's experiences and gathered and offer to you this collection of poems as my gift - a bouquet of life.

Thank you for choosing to read my thoughts. I hope and pray that they will continually entertain, encourage and refresh you each time you join me on the meadow.

Paul Ray

To see the world in a grain of sand
and heaven in a wildflower,
hold infinity in the palm of your hand
and eternity in an hour.

WILLIAM BLAKE

[1757-1827]

Flowering Meadows

At Last With Fall

What beauty comes at last with Fall
When golden hour is best of all -
Where Autumn's light set trees aglow
With shimmering shades and bright yellow,
And where each backdrop's reddish scene
Is sprinkled with some evergreen.

It seems to be a magic sign
When colors clash against the pine,
And temperatures begin to change
While verdant hillsides rearrange.

It's when there's splendor by a lake,
And when there's piles of leaves to rake;
There're pumpkin patches plain in view,
And frost that chills each morning dew.

What beauty comes at last with Fall
When sunflowers grow up nice and tall,
And sway in fields where asters grow
With purple heads lined in a row -
Where butterflies swim in the air,
And dance amongst the clover there.

There's wonder in a mountain scene
With quilt-like colors in between
The peaks, the ranges, and the sky
Where downy cotton clouds drift by.

There're crisp clean chills felt in each breeze
While gently fall the sun scorched leaves;
An amber tinge to morning's haze,
And maple leaves glow with a blaze.

What beauty comes at last with Fall
As God repaints His earthen ball
With touches made with red and gold?
It is a wonder to behold.
But though I'm no authority -
I know God did this all for me.

Know My Heart Still Lies In You

If God should call me first my love,
Then know my heart still lies in you;
I'll always be right there my dove
To share in all the things you do.
In every bright and sunlit day -
While God sends you His fresh warm air;
I'll be in every beam and ray
That lands upon your face and hair.
Or when the rain falls to your feet
That bathes each flower or fills each brook
I'll be in all the pools you meet
That shimmer from each loving look.
And every night while you're in bed,
Before your dreams begin to grow;
I'll listen to each prayer that's said,
While letting all my kisses flow.
My love for you is full and deep -
It spans beyond the farthest sea;
Remember this before you sleep...
And know someday you'll fly with me.

A Man Has Died For You Today

A man has died for you today -
He could have stopped,
And walked away;
And left you there in rags of gray -
With filth from all your sin.

He was a man with simple clothes -
Who walked with dirt
Between His toes;
And common as appearance goes -
With dark and weathered skin.

This man built tables, stands and chair -
With sawdust often
In His hair;
A skill his Father taught Him there
While He was growing up.

But though this man learned little trade -
He gave you hope
When there He laid
Upon a cross in pain and stayed
To drink your bitter cup.

A man has died for you today -
Remember this
In work and play,
And of His resurrection day
Which ties you both to Him.

And while you wear new clothes of white -
Rejoice and praise
The God of Light;
Who gave His son to you, despite
The rags that you were in.

Just Like Bread

With a lot of little lovin' -
As with bread baked in the oven;
After time we'll watch hearts rising
If our lives aren't compromising;
Serving others, filled with laughter,
And consistent ever after.
We'll lift souls when love is spread -
Just like being yeast in bread.

From a passionate plead while praying -
Like a child, we start by saying,
"Please God help me be like Jesus,
When the fear to do right freezes;
Help me love those who are hateful,
And be kind to the ungrateful."
With such prayers God's Kingdom's led -
Just by being broken bread.

Through small gifts of Godly giving -
All the time here while we're living,
We drop crumbs for folks to swallow;
When they do, they'll come and follow -
Being drawn to God's true blessing,
Seen in us - they'll come confessing,
And be joined in Christ, well fed -
Just from eating of His bread.

First Snow Watch

Slow and softly snowflakes land
On my outstretched tongue and hand;
While I gaze with great delight,
As first snow cloaks all in white.

From the stillness of my stance
I hear wind while crystals dance;
Watching flakes from frigid skies
Fall intact or vaporize.

Sparkling crystalline shapes abound,
Drop, then drape without a sound;
Making outlines smooth and clean -
Now made bright and quite pristine.

Winter's magic comes to share
Her ice show of powdered air;
Cold and gentle to the touch -
Marvelous dream I love so much.

Daughter's Prayer

As fire and light are sinking low,
While peace and quiet fill the air;
I kneel beside my child's pillow,
And listen to her tender prayer.

With gentle voice to God she speaks,
As if He's next to her in bed;
And tells Him how she joyfully seeks
To be with Him on high, instead.

She prays with thanks for gifts unseen -
For wisdom that He gives each day;
And thanks the Lord for all who've been
A source of strength along the way.

Oh precious child, who causes tears
To flow like streams along my face;
I see you're wise beyond your years -
For seeking aid through God's embrace.

The child of mine begins to end,
With prayers for folks she's thinking of;
And also asks that God will mend
Her selfish ways and show more love.

At that I hear her say, "Amen,"
Then wrapping her in quilt and sheet;
I kiss her head and rise again
To let her rest at Jesus' feet.

Harry Higgins Hollingsworth

Harry Higgins Hollingsworth
Had a problem with his girth
He would sit in larger chairs
And at school sometimes in pairs
Though his size caused some reaction
Hard work brought him satisfaction
And his grades spread a reaction
To the teachers of his school
Showing he was no one's fool.

Wearing jerseys was his style
With his laughter and his smile
Never absent, never late
Never spoke a word of hate
He would sling his bag on shoulders
Filled with books that felt like boulders
Everyday with notes in folders
To each class prepared to learn
Raising hand to speak in turn.

Late one night while in his room
Harry heard a loud "ka-boom"
And, because of this, he woke
Hearing screams he smelled some smoke
Running with the flames on ceiling
Harry grabbed his Mom while reeling
From the fumes and fire then peeling
Out of house with Mom secure
Then inside for Dad he tore.

Fire was spreading all around
Timbers falling to the ground
Hair was singeing from the heat
As the youngster moved his feet
Looking fast while coughing badly
Harry screamed for his dad madly
Then he saw his father sadly
Laying on a burning bed
He grabbed him and then he fled.

All his school learned in a flash
Harry's house burned up in ash
Out of school - all burned and bruised
His school absence was excused
All survived because of Harry
Who risked all and did not tarry
Even though the flames were scary
Well known now in size and heart...
Along with him being smart.

Commit To the Lord Your Plans

When work begins I always ask
The Lord for guidance in each task,
And know great gain is certain when
I humbly doff my prideful mask.

Though I may have the knowledge in
The job at hand as I begin;
Without a selfless servant heart,
My efforts will result in sin.

No matter what the craft or art,
My skill or gift will come apart,
If I don't first commit my plans
To Him on High before I start.

For God has said each map of mans
Will find success on seas and lands,
If they are first laid in His hands,
If they are first laid in His hands.

Thank You For The Flowers

Thank you for the flowers
That you send with love and care;
And for your special friendship
Which God gave us both to share.

All your gifts are precious ones -
We both simply adore;
Like getting bags of vegetables
You lay next to our door.

Every time we walk and talk -
You give a word of cheer;
To brighten us and fill us up
With joy throughout the year.

Thank you for your thoughtfulness
In all the things you do;
We both are blessed to know two souls
As wonderful as you.

Help Me To Shine God

Good morning God
So great and wise
Help me to shine
Before your eyes
Let me be used
This day to share
Your hope and peace
As answered prayer
Help guide my steps
To meet a need
And may your words
Be mine in deed
May those I greet
And help this day
All feel the love
You give away
And most of all
Let people see
The way to Christ
As you use me
Please help me show
The joy you give
With trusting faith
So they can live.

Tongue Training

Sometimes when I am cross and tired
From over work when those that hired
Me to replace some folks who made
The problem worse through escapades;
I say a word or phrase in haste
That I at once would like erased -
So I could start all over then,
And not feel guilt from words of sin.

Each poison word can kill a flame,
Or destroy dreams so none remain
Inside the hearts of young and old
To cause their passions to run cold;
For every hurtful word in jest
Can haunt and harm the heart at best,
And make one think how things would be
If words were spoken more kindly.

The tongue is just a mirror part
That shows what's deep inside the heart,
And must be trained not to lash back
When tempers tempt us to attack;
For when the tongue is tamed and tight,
And used for God, it shines a light -
Which spreads and heals the hearts of men
So they can rise and live again.

Bed Battles

On top of the covers that layered young Ben
Were colorful soldiers all painted and tin;
They stood in formations with cannons all poised,
While captains rode horseback and drummers made noise.
The banners of each army waved in the breeze
With soldiers at hilltops made up of Ben's knees;
And there on a plain soldiers lined down below
On a cotton white field formed by Ben's soft pillow.

Each man was placed slowly - with strategies made
To gain good position and send their brigade
Through the hills of Ben's feet and o'er the crest of his toes -
While battalions would move toward the flag of their foes.
Some would fall, it was certain; some would lose their command,
From a cannon ball blast or the wave of Ben's hand;
But a victor would rise through the volley and fire
When one side caused the flag they opposed to retire.

Ben's bed brightly bristled with horses and men,
While a strange creaking sound from outside came within;
All waited with courage - their cue to commence,
As onslaughts would follow with battles intense.
Then the moment did come - each commander raised sword,
And the drummers began beating all in accord;
As the cannons were pounding and as all gave a shout -
Then suddenly Spike the dog stamped it all out.

Live Thee This Day

Live thee this day to walk with thy God -
Committed to die as ye follow;
Swift be the drink with thy feet to each want -
Sooth and refresh at each swallow.

Purposely place thyself down at one's feet -
Bathing each soul with compassion;
Gently caress with thy kisses and tears -
Tend in a Christ-loving fashion.

Seek not to gain from benevolence shared -
God loves when gifts are well-hidden;
Serve Him with fervor and joy in thy heart -
Teach from Christ's words what is written.

Live thee this day to walk with thy God -
Encourage with love those before thee;
Walk in a way each can follow Christ home -
Joining again in God's glory.

A Blanket Lullaby

Snuggle up beneath your blanket
Warm yourself in linen sheet;
As you do, the angels gather -
Kissing both your head and feet.

Lay your head down on your pillow
Close your eyes and dream tonight;
God is here and loves you deeply
Holding you in radiant light.

Holy, precious child of heaven
Rest in peace - the day is through;
You are blessed beyond all measure
As the stars look down on you.

Drift, dear one, on silk and slumber
Catch a boat on silvery streams;
God will steer your vessel safely
Through the moonlight of your dreams.

When you wake again tomorrow
With your dinghy safe at bay;
Know that God will never leave you
As He sends you on your way.

Good Morning Sweet Sunshine

Good morning sweet sunshine -
How warm are your rays;
Your shine is a savior
After rain all these days.

Your light brings a splendor
To mist on the grass;
While webs on the trees
Glisten gently like glass.

The streams and the lakes
All shimmer like gold;
And the flowers are fragrant
As they stretch and unfold.

The dove gives a call,
And the chickadees, too;
As they sing their sweet song
With a greeting to you.

"Good morning," they sing,
"Thank you for your bright face;
We are glad that you're back
Bringing warmth to this place."

Then a gentle breeze comes,
And they all fly away;
But your glow carries on
As the source of the day.

From A Room Down Our Hallway

There's a room down our hallway
On the northwestern side,
That has rarely been entered
With its door opened wide.
It is locked all the time
With no keyhole to peer;
But I'm sure things are growing
Inside that I fear.
Late at night the walls shake
From a low booming noise;
While a voice screams with laughter,
"Don't mess with my toys!"
Then some footsteps are heard
Running fast on the floor -
With an, "Ooo!" and a "No!"
And a slam of a door.

Later on the next morning
When all banshees have fled,
I come up to that doorway
To waken the dead.
With some guts and some courage
I knock the door thrice,
And I say, "Time to get up!"
Though fuming, I'm nice.
Then comes some gurgling
From inside that room;
Like a lava pit monster
Returning from doom.
Then a soft speaking voice
Sweetly charms me with ease;
"Daddy, I love you -
Now go away please."

Hell Talk

Hell's not a favorite topic taught
In church and Sunday school;
Because it is the opposite
Outside God's heavenly rule.

It's pictured as a fiery pit
Filled with the bad below;
That disobeyed the living God -
To feed their own ego.

Most people cringe to think about
The horror of that place;
Where souls forever agonize
With torment on each face.

There Satan holds each soul in pain
With laughter loud and shrill;
And burns them for his own pleasure
To gratify his will.

With that in mind, just realize
He's after your soul, too;
He'll lie and make things sound so good
To keep the truth from you.

"Just sit around and do not serve -
Don't bother to believe.
You are not lost!" He says to you,
While trying to deceive.

When you hear that, you need to say,
"Get lost you evil one!
Our lives are not our own, but God's -
Forever in His son."

So stand and share, and trust in God
To live and serve Him well;
And through our Lord we'll help each soul
Escape the fires of hell.

Sleep Little Owlet

Sweet little owlet, tuck under your wings
Sleep in your nest of soft moss, twigs and strings;
High in an oak tree you perch and you peek
Rocked by the wind that blows under your beak.
Time for the stars to fade out and be gone
Time for some warmth from the sun at the dawn.
Rest there my woodland child, bask in its glow
Safe and secure from the beasts down below.
Dream now of large fish all swimming in pools
Where you swoop down plucking one from their schools.
Then you go dining high up in the trees
Spreading your pinions, enjoying the breeze;
Gracefully gliding and soaring along
Hunting nocturnally while hooting your song.
Slumber sweet owlet, the night, it has past
Cling to your mother while sweet moments last
Soon will the sun set and stars will shine bright
Again you can spread wings, then leap to take flight.

A Simply Cool Treat

No matter what the weather's like
In Winter or in Spring;
My wife just loves when I bring home
A cold and simple thing.

It's found at certain places
Which are hard sometimes to find;
But always makes her cheer right up
With a happy frame of mind.

I carry it in plastic bags
Away from heat and sun;
For if I let it get exposed
My good deed gets undone.

Once purchased, I must hasten home
To freeze it once again;
As planning is the key to keep
A mess from happenin'.

Sometimes, when I am traveling
And in a diner seat;
I hear its sound scooped in a glass
To serve folks while they eat.

Or when I'm at the carnival
A vendor hands out cones;
With cherry-lemon topped liqueur
Atop their frosty thrones.

The sound it makes is wonderful
When dropped straight in a cup;
From fridge or fancy ice machine
To chill a drink right up.

But nothing's more rewarding and
No pleasure will suffice;
To make my sweetheart happy
Than a bag of cold crushed ice.

Seek Him All Your Years

I'm watching now my precious one
As you fall fast asleep;
I kiss you on your gentle brow
While angels 'round you keep.
God's love for you surpasses Great,
Which often brings me tears;
I pray that you will grow in God -
And seek Him all your years.

I'll do my best, sweet child of mine
To raise you strong and brave;
You'll learn respect and discipline,
And the ways to behave.
With patient love I'll be your guide
As you grow up with peers;
I'll pray you choose to follow God -
And seek Him all your years.

There'll be a day, I hope far off,
When death will pound life's door;
You'll feel the ache from loss and grief -
A pain you have in store.
But since you're just a babe right now
With no taste of life's fears;
I'll pray that you will trust in God -
And seek Him all your years.

And when I die and leave this earth
With you knelt by my side;
I'll hope to watch you from above
Filled with a Father's pride.
For there I hope you'll live for Christ
In service, love and cheers;
While helping others come to God -
You'll seek Him all your years.

The Poetic Way To Rid A Satirist

Some satirists will often rise
Who'll love to poke and trash with lies
Some poetry each hates and tries
To bury in the sand.

For in the past they'd take a verse
Of poet's work, then they'd rehearse,
And twist it 'round to form a curse
To mock it as their plan.

If it were Poe with valentine
Who'd sent his love a verse so fine,
Where critics stole and changed each line
To make his lady sore -

He'd promptly learn what they had done,
And print their names up in "The Sun"
As scoundrels read by everyone;
A problem - nevermore.

Gnarly Snarly Goosebump Green

Gnarly snarly Goosebump Green
Meanest man that ever was seen;
Lived alone on top of a hill
In a shack next to the landfill.

He would rarely go to town -
When he did, he'd cuss and he'd frown;
Scared the ladies out of there wits
When he used the sidewalk for spits.

Never warm - without a friend
Handshake never did he extend;
Sat on porch, while grumpy all day -
Scaring folks that might come his way.

If ever someone walked by
Goosebump Green would yell and then cry,
"Git your hiney off a my lan'!"
Making noise by banging a pan.

This went on for years and years -
Goosebump grumbled, throwing out sneers;
'Til, one day, some kids happened by -
Seeing Green on steps where he lie.

Straight away they ran to Green
Even though they knew he was mean;
They called out but he just laid still -
Checking pulse they found he was ill.

Medics came, changed the heart rate
Of a man most easy to hate;
So, by kindness shown there with haste
Goosebump Green's life was not erased.

Over time Goosebump did change -
Cause of youth, who helped rearrange
His past life from a tangled mess;
Now he winks with true thankfulness.

The Rabbit In My Garden

Early in the morning hours
I went out to pick some flowers
In my garden, near the woodshed
Where a rabbit sat in my bed
Munching, crunching on a daisy
Sitting there and looking lazy
But when he saw my two eyes -
I knew we were both surprised.

All at once he did a big flip
Rolling on a Danish tulip
Flopping, hopping in my garden
Chattering, "I beg your pardon"
While he pounced through my Hibiscus
With his paws and long white whiskas
Looking for a simple path
To escape my growing wrath.

As I neared the raised bed siding
He dove under Poppies, hiding
Waiting there with his heart beating
Hoping we would not be meeting
Anymore with startled faces
If excused by my good graces
Quiet now he sat in fear
Knowing I was ever near.

At that moment I decided
To be kind as wrath subsided
Knowing rabbits were God's creatures
That I learned from Bible teachers
There I stood near hidden bunny
Who did not think this was funny
As I thought, "What would God do?"
In my heart I quickly knew.

After that I showed compassion
Kicking dirt in noisy fashion
Which caused rabbit to run quickly
Through some roses that were prickly
Toward his freedom past the fencing
Which I knew he now was sensing
As I watched each rabbit ear
Zip to wood then disappear.

My Father's In My Father's Arms

My Father's in my Father's arms -
He's gone to Heaven now;
His clothes are white,
They shine with light -
A crown sits on his brow.

Triumphant is his entry there -
While angels sing with praise;
The streets, I'm told,
Are purest gold,
That he'll tread all his days.

My Father's there with Christ the King -
They're walking side by side;
He's home at last,
Where pain has passed,
And only peace abides.

He's kissed by all his family
Who've longed in wait for him;
They greet him there
With love and care -
So glad he's home again.

My Father's space smells heavenly -
Sweet fragrance fills the halls;
For in his room
Great roses bloom
On corridors and walls.

And on his loft there is a chair
With cello, bow and stands;
Where now he plays,
Both nights and days,
Great music with his hands.

My Father's in my Father's house -
Forever now above;
He's in that place
Because of grace
Shared by God's son with love.

I hope some day to hold him close -
To meet him in the skies;
And once again
Be joined with him,
And see his bright blue eyes.

The Birth Of Our Boy

In the late morning hours
On the eleventh of May,
Came a bundle of joy
That brought sunshine our way.
There was tension at first
When our babe was first born;
For he swallowed some stuff
That clogged lungs up that morn.
The docs moved around fast,
Helping child start to breathe;
And when he did cry
We were both so relieved.
It was then that we heard
The most beautiful sound;
Like the voice of an angel
Who was singing face down.
His cry soothed us both,
As we held him at last -
In a warm soft blanket
That transcended the past.
We could see his eyes squint
As we counted his toes;
And we saw where an angel
Placed a kiss on his nose.
I hummed in his ear
The Brahms Lullaby,
As I cuddled the apple,
And joy of my eye.
Then my wife and I prayed -
Thanking God for His bliss,
And for the gift of a son
Both to love and to kiss.

Christmas Mall Magic

While standing in a crowded mall
At Christmas time where trees are tall -
I see where wreaths are hung with care
As sparkling lights shine everywhere.
There's gingerbread and candy canes
And Teddy bears through frosted panes -
Where gifts and treats are all for sale
In crowded shops where babies wail.
I hear what every merchant sells
As Santa rings donation bells
And watch the people in their coats
Wear hats and scarves around their throats.
Some shiny bags have gifts all wrapped
And parents have their shoulders tapped
By children asking for a hint
Of what could be in each present.
The registers around me ring
As people stand in line to bring
Their credit cards and cash to buy
A Mom a vase or Dad a tie.
The hurry and the rush is seen
On many folks, both old and teen.
Yet, even though so many run,
I often see a kindness done -
Sometimes a person without cause
Transforms into a Santa Claus
While bringing joy to someone's face
Which brightens those around the place.
But there's a gift, I'll share what's true -
God sent His son for me and you -
His name is said throughout the mall
And brings true joy to one and all.

jane

Sister fair
With loving care -
You give from God's own heart.

Precious jewel
From God's own rule -
You serve with divine art.

Lovely child
Of God so mild -
Who gently holds and mends.

Holy one
Saved by God's son -
With love that never ends.

Joyful saint
Who loves to paint -
Your sunshine smile is sweet.

Friend to all
That hears God call -
You love each one you meet.

Star of light
Who speaks what's right -
From God's Word all your days.

Slave on earth
With noble birth -
God calls your name with praise.

A Promise Made

A promise made should not be treated lightly -
An oath or pledge should not be left undone;
When given, grab the reins and hold on tightly
To stay on course until its race is run.

To carelessly commit when not intended,
Or swear with fingers crossed to make amends;
May run off love or those whom we've befriended,
And leave us in our lives with fewer friends.

The truth be known - integrity is lapsing
In schools and businesses abroad each day;
And, with so many marriages collapsing -
It shows that even vows have gone astray.

So, with so many promises now broken
In years gone by, and in the present, too;
May we be ones whose honor is unspoken
Because we do what we say we will do.

I'm Not One Now

No, I'm not one who'll live my years
With deep regrets, "what ifs," and fears
Of never spending time at home
Where love abounds and children roam.
For there the treasures of my heart
Keep holding me as I depart
To go about my work each day -
Because God blessed me in this way.
For every morn my wife will hold
Me in her arms till we unfold
With one great kiss that tides us through
Till we're both home with young ones too.

No, I'm not one who'll seldom write
To thank, to love, to bless or spite,
And with no purpose, pass the time;
Instead I often write in rhyme.
For letters mailed with pure intent
To lift a soul are heaven sent.
They are the gifts that last through years
As folded parchments stained with tears.
They're jewels clutched to a mother's breast;
They're lights that shine where inmates rest;
They're arms that lift a soldier's side,
And hugs where homeless people hide.

No, I'm not one who'll walk away
When there's a need that comes my way;
Or look to find an easy out
When I'm inclined to lie about.
Because through Christ I've learned to care
For others hurting in despair.
God took me in; I'm now on earth
To share Christ's wondrous hope and mirth
With everyone around my sphere
While showing love that casts out fear.
And it's my hope in Christ they'll be -
One day adopted, just like me.

Heels Of Bread

How many times have you just thrown away
The heels in a bag of bread?
The ends of each loaf
You gather, and both
Are broken to make the birds fed.

What makes the heel such an unwanted thing
That children and grownups dislike?
Is dryness the key
Or texture, maybe -
So we trash it, or give it a spike?

Maybe it's just how we view the whole thing
That formed in a youthful brain -
We thought as a child
The heel was just styled
As a shell to protect the whole grain.

We left that image of shell in our mind
'Til we have a natural view -
That heels are the waste
On loaves, so in haste
We discard them before they turn blue.

Are we not heels in the sight of our God
As scraps just to be tossed aside?
But His love divine
Serves us up with wine
When we follow Him home to abide.

I Hear A Jingle Jangle

I hear a jingle jangle
From bells on horse and sleigh,
And see a single candle
In lamp that lights our way.
Our faithful steed Sir Morris
Pulls sled along the snow,
As family sings in chorus -
"To Grandma's house we go."
The winter air is biting
While flakes frolic and swirl;
The singing is delighting
My covered wife and girl.
Though dark and half past seven,
As hooves stamp to a beat;
We'll soon be home, like heaven,
Where family's kiss and greet.
The winter's downy motion
Makes paths all soft and white,
As I steer with devotion
To stay on course at night.
And soon, far in the distance,
Where lights begin to shine;
We'll glide without resistance
To pumpkin, ham and wine.

Nighty Night And Twinkle Toes

Nighty Night and Twinkle Toes
Greet every child with nightly shows
Of yawning mouths and rubbing eyes,
While hair is brushed and baths arise.

Each brings a gift to child in bed,
After they're tucked and prayers are said;
And when they're kissed with doors closed tight,
The gifts begin with Nighty Night.

Tippietoe comes Nighty Night,
With wondrous magic for a sprite;
He brings to children pleasant dreams,
With puppy, kitten, lambkin themes.

There, children roam in fields of gold
With furry friends for each to hold.
They laugh with others all the day;
While filled with love and joy, they play.

The skies are blue, the trees are green -
Both air and water's crystal clean;
For through these dreams of peace and joy,
He blesses every girl and boy.

And while they dream and scratch their nose,
Who should appear but Twinkle Toes!
Oh Twinkle Toes; He comes at last,
And brings a gift of memories past.

With pleasant thoughts, the children see
The love they have from family;
With visions sweet of days gone by
Of picnic plates and pumpkin pie.

There're times with Grandpa on his boat,
And times with Auntie and her goat;
There're times of holding Mama tight and
Times with Pa flying a kite.

Each child sees friends in dreamland, too,
Who inspire them by what they do.
They're preachers, teachers, friends at school,
And neighbor kids they think are cool.

Most children dream with thoughts of these,
The gift that Twinkle Toes bequeaths;
But as each child wakes to morn's light -
Away goes Twink' and Nighty Night.

In Memory Of Our Heroes

I placed my hands on a gravestone
Of a soldier down a white line;
Who had died in the heat of battle
In "Operation Watch on the Rhine."

I saw where etched in the marble
His soul was committed to God;
A hero of men and all nations
Now resting in peace under sod.

A flood of tears came o'er me
As I saw him rush in the snow;
From a foxhole close to Bastogne
With a wind chill near fifteen below.

There he was with no thought of peril
Covering ground in ice and the mire;
With grenades he took out some gunmen
And machine guns with heavy fire.

But then a Tiger tank bellowed
That blasted the snow through the wind;
And as the snow dust had settled
All knew it was this man's end.

There I stood in awe of his valor
There I wept while moved by his grit;
For I knew he never once cowered
As he fought with honor through it.

Then I looked at all the white crosses
That had lined the fields and the hills;
Of the heroes lost in their battles
That gave up their wants and their wills.

So to all who've served our great nation
Both enlisted and the veterans, too;
For the duty and way that you serve us
I respect and salute all of you.

Book Worms

Jasmine and Jeremy loved to read
A book every night at amazing speed;
They'd lie on their bed
Or sit in a chair -
Reading book after book after book right there.

Books in their room would be on the floor
All sorted by author, by topic and more;
Then next to their bed
Were books that were new -
With pile after pile after pile to view.

Stories of Sinbad and Dorian Gray,
Stories by Wells, Poe and Hemingway;
The fantasies shelved,
The histories on racks -
With page after page after page of facts.

Jasmine and Jeremy loved to read
And together one day did a marvelous deed;
They gave of their time
At a nursing home -
And read and they read and they read book and poem.

The folks loved the reading of both these two,
And the more they read then the more they knew
That their love of books
Was just a start -
For the tear after tear after tear changed their heart.

He Will

If you can't go to sleep due to worry,
Or you can't go to sleep due to fear;
Then it's time to give God all your burdens -
HE will make every one disappear.

If your focus in life seems distorted,
And your purpose some how seems concealed;
Then it's time to ask God for directions -
HE will make your best path be revealed.

HE will...
Take your problems, take your cares
Take your hate and take away your tears in pairs
Take your grief and take your sin...
For God wants you to be with Him.

If resentment is hurting a friendship,
And you want to avoid, scream or pout;
Then it's time to let God work inside you -
HE will help to resolve it all out.

If possessions are latched to your heart strings,
And you've placed this or that before Him;
Then it's time to let God do some changing -
HE will help you prioritize them.

HE will...
Take your problems, take your cares
Take your hate and take away a few gray hairs
Take your grief and take your sin...
For God wants you to be with him.

Key To A Successful Misadventure

Recently a grown up lad
Went rushing with the clothes he had
To catch a plane at morning's light -
That took off towards his college site.

But while he rested in the air
A cockpit pane crack caused despair;
Which forced his plane to be brought down
To a great country music town.

It's there he waited in a seat
While listening to the country beat
Of Krauss, Black, Jennings and the Judds
On an iTouch with his earbuds.

This seemed to pass the time away
While being stuck with a delay
Of reaching his objective place -
Though some frustration crossed his face.

But while he heard "Alyssa Lies"
His father called with a surprise;
Who said he'd left car keys behind -
Which made "Good grief!" be his next line.

Still, with this news, he kept his cool,
For he had friend with keys at school -
Who, when called, said he'd drive the key
And meet him at his SUV.

Then green light came to mended craft
With all things checked from nose to aft;
Which flew and landed safely where
He met his friend with car key spare.

With greetings and a "How are you?"
He thanked his friend for his rescue;
Then back to school both drove the route
While thanking God it all worked out.

Through A Loss

A loss at first floods feelings of despair
With inward bouts of self affliction;
Through time of grief and constant prayer
God heals by His own benediction -
But tenderly, frequently flow the tears
In coming years.

Each time a favorite word or phrase is said -
Each time a gift exchange is met with laughter;
In every note their hands wrote down is read,
And every closet with their things filled to the rafter -
The memories, constantly come and go
Like winds that blow.

Their voice may fade as time keeps streaming on -
Though sounds from them will never die completely;
New dreams will come since they have passed and gone,
And joy will fill the days again while sweetly -
We longingly wait, through time and space
For their embrace.

A Question

Simply swiftly ticks the time
Life is brief with shorter prime
Moments come and moments go
Some to cherish, some to grow
Start as infant, child then teen
Simple, sage and in between
Schooled and taught throughout the years
How to act and serve one's peers
Job, house, wedding, baby's sound
As the cycle comes around
Then retirement, then to lie
There in bed hooked up to die.
Just one thought as doors close shut -
After death takes hold...then what?

One Special Cellist

Cello sounds in all its glory
Played with bow from E. Sartory
Pouring, singing rich with passion
To his God in angel fashion
Raising, lifting songs to heaven
With a gift this soul was given
Playing strings with warm vibrato
Slurring notes in smooth legato
Tones that bless angelic highways
Bringing joy to souls on byways
There in perfect light forever
Sings the cello and the giver
Who on earth has blessed some men
But now for God he'll never end.

Ixannaq

There was a dog named Ixannaq
Whose eyes were white and spooky;
He lived inside a drainage ditch
On Elm in Chattanoogie.
He'd been a stray for three long weeks
When speedin' caused some trouble;
His master died when truck flipped 'round
Which threw him into rubble.
Sweet Ixannaq was beautiful
Though fur was smudged and musty;
And one fine day he visited
A girl who cried out, "Husky!"
This was a dream for Sally Ann
To see a dog sit 'side her;
Since she was sick and wheelchair-bound
This dog made Sally brighter.
As Sally pulled the collar close
Which Ixannaq was wearing;
She tried to read it properly
Though struggling while staring.
Then Sally called her Mom to see
The guest who'd come to dinner;
And when her Mom saw Ixannaq
She knew he was a winner.
She dialed the dog tag's phone number
As fast as she was able;
But when she found the phone cut off
She made signs at the table.
Though signs were posted everywhere
Nobody ever called back;
And soon young Sally and her Mom
Had dog they both called "Ixnak."

Ixannaq (Its-zan-nak) is an Inuit word for "friend."

God Hugs

Everybody needs compassion
In the flesh, while pressing tight;
Love is more than words of comfort
Touching sheds a different light.

Soft and slow the hand caresses -
Wiping face, erasing tears;
Sweetly sharing love while silent -
Smoothing out life's troubling years.

Gentle strokes across the forehead -
Kisses placed from cheek to cheek;
Massage rubs along the shoulders -
These are presents people seek.

Just remember from our childhoods
That we all need hugs to live;
It's shown first while in our cradles
With the love our parents give.

We are children of the Master -
Each unique in life and view;
And He hopes that all will seek Him
To be raised and cherished, too.

Fingers reaching to be lifted -
Hands all clinging to His waist;
Feet and toes spring elevated -
Jumping up and down with haste.

Faces smiling, bright and cheerful
While hands poke and push and prod;
Hoping for the greatest moment -
To be held and hugged by God.

Classroom Valentines

Early in my years at school
I'd bring box for V-Day's pool;
Where the carton brought would hold
Valentines both creased and rolled.
There my box was renovated,
Papered, glued and decorated,
With the top part separated;
Labeled and placed next to coats -
Waiting to be filled with notes.

Words of love were carefully placed,
And our cards perfumed or laced;
Trimmed with hearts up to the hilt -
Of construction paper built.
Then each child would quickly fold them,
And get up to wedge or mold them
In each box with hooks to hold them;
To be opened one and all -
On V-Day at teacher's call.

Then on day with memory -
Teacher let us all go see
What we found in our own box;
Hoping not to just find rocks.
All at once there came a giggle,
Girls would smile and boys would wiggle,
And a few would jump or tickle
When some faces turned maroon -
As I watched one girl just swoon.

Missing Daddy

Just when things were going right
Corporate needed Dad's insight
So they booked him on a flight
To a conference late one night
Leaving kids and wife so pretty
To a town called New York City
Family liked it - not one bitty
Since that week they'd have no Dad
And would leave their mommy sad.

Through the week the phone calls came
Speaking to each one by name
Sharing love to each his aim
Though it wasn't quite the same
When their pets showed growls or hissing
Children shared their hurts while missing
All their Daddy's hugs and kissing
Hoping to be held real soon
Each one wished this night and noon.

Then one eve with peaceful hive
As the clocks turned eight-o-five
Shining lights pulled in the drive
Making kids all come alive
Faces peeking by the sashes
Quickly jumped with tearful lashes
Running with their feet in dashes
Out from under roof and dome
Screaming loudly, "Daddy's home!"

The Sunrise Painter

When the night is transformed by daylight,
And the sun crests over the sea;
It's a time of anticipation
For a new work of God's artistry.

At the dawn come light beams in glory
That shoot out and stretch overhead;
Where the rays cause clouds to start glowing
While the Lord paints them all pink or red.

Later on the heavens shoot fireworks,
And the ocean below shines in white;
There's a beauty about it eternal
That's a glimpse for God's children of light.

In the sky and through the aurora
Come the call and the birds of the air;
It is God who puts them on canvas
As He purposely places them there.

For the God of all paints every landscape
With His love as He colors each view;
Look around and see all His brush strokes,
And remember that He painted you.

For each dawn is a gift from the Father,
Shared with hues in majestic array;
It should be on the top of our prayer list
As we thank Him for His art display.

Clearing Land In Limones

I aided in the clearing of tall brush and jagged briar
On land beyond a pitted lane of dust and humid heat;
Machete blades all glistened as our stacks of hedge grew higher
While prickly burrs adjoined our legs and feet.

The orange and the lemon trees gave shade in one location -
But not enough to shield the rays that beat upon our brows;
We picked and dug a drainage hole till rock produced frustration -
Then stopping, we all went to Xandro's house.

We hopped in vans and pickup trucks with mud-caked quarter panels,
And held on tight while driving over trenched and rocky ground;
The radios were blasting, tuned to Spanish-singing channels,
While all enjoyed the loud Latino sound.

The drive through Limones was slow, with no signs I could follow -
Where homes were built with random block and roofs were made of thatch;
Each house had water in a drum to wash, to bathe or swallow,
And every wall could use some paint or patch.

When finally we got to rest, the women served burritos -
All topped with spicy peppers which brought fire to my dried lips;
I quickly downed some orange juice and grabbed up some Doritos,
And ate them with some avocado dips.

Then after lunch we thanked our hosts for meals cooked in their kettle,
And went back to the site to work where a new church would be;
I got stabbed by some thorns and thought of Christ's past crown of nettle -
That helped me have a sense of Calvary.

When brambles on the land were cleared, we had a family showing,
And all the church in town did come to gather and to pray;
We asked the Lord to bless His church where building would be going,
With hopes it would bring praise to Him each day.

Now I look back at that great trip where I thought I was giving,
But found that I was given more from hearts that shared with me;
The people there in Limones are great in Godly living -
They blessed my life with rich humility.

Dad's Simple Manger Scene

In every December when trees weren't so green,
My father would build a nativity scene;
In front of his house, and close to a stair,
Dad set up a frame and a manger scene there.

He'd lay out three figures that lit up in white -
With Mary and Joseph and babe glowing bright;
And down on the ground, and where the babe lay,
My father would always spread out some fresh hay.

When done, he'd clean up all the boxes and bags,
And put them away next to wreaths and some rags;
Then staring in awe of a world changing view,
He thanked God for Jesus who made him anew.

"Three figures?" I once asked, "Why Dad, only three?
Where are the shepherds and sheep gazing free?
Where are the kings that had traveled afar?
Where are Melchior, Balthasar and Gaspar?"

"Where is the great star that arose from the East?
Where is its great light guiding men to true peace?
And where are the angels that came from the sky?
Why are these all left out? Dad, please tell me why?"

At those words my father looked at me and said,
"Son, those are great moments from God's word you've read;
But learn just to focus on the main event -
When God became flesh - man's redemption was sent."

Feline Flexing

Velvet ears twitch on the landing -
Whiskers glow from rays of light;
Paws of felt stretch wide while handing
Out pink pads with claws of white.

Mouth gapes high under compulsion -
Showing tongue with fangs and teeth;
Stirring up a quick convulsion
As my feline gets relief.

Hind legs rise as tail shoots upward -
Rump goes up as head's near ground;
Front hooks scratch a close by cupboard
With his clawing kitty sound.

After that my friend starts purring -
As he curls back up to sleep;
Then his dreams start up their stirring
While he rests without a peep.

A Menagerie Of Imagery

Slimy squid on mashed potatoes
Liver served with green tomatoes
Broken glass that cut up eight toes;
Not a pretty sight.

Lollypops and candied apples
Tug of war with wrestling grapples
Bells that ring in country chapels;
Fun and a delight.

Children sick impoverished dying
Soldiers at a gravesite crying
Diplomats corrupt from lying;
Seldom hit the news.

Champions raise their gold elated
Movies in the papers rated and
Violence in our schools all stated;
Where are our values?

Images like these stir feelings
Some disgusting, some bring healings
Others make us hit our ceilings
With our rage inside.

Though we all have much emotion
Let's learn to restrain the notion
To start hateful thoughts in motion,
And let love abide.

Family values not held dearer
Monitors inside our mirror
Prejudice still ever nearer;
These cause quite a scare.

But warm embraces shown and tearful
Tender words that heal the fearful
Loving acts while daily prayerful;
These we need to share.

At the Coffee Shop

There in hand with cup of coffee,
I stirred in some caramel toffee;
At a kiosk of a vendor
Who exchanges drinks for tender.
As I breathed in caffeine vapors,
I glanced down at morning papers;
During which I lounged in chair -
Soothed by smells of java there.

Looking at the rolls for buying
At a level right for spying,
While I sipped my roast with pleasure,
I saw Danish Crèmes - a treasure!
So I quickly placed an order
That I bought with bill and quarter;
Then in turn with brew and bun
I sat down to eat - 'til done.

As I sat, I heard some chatter -
People talking through the clatter;
Orders made with blenders turning,
Crushing ice as froth was churning.
Lattes, black and cappuccinos,
Demitasse or frappuccinos;
Hot and cold to meet each need -
All served up at lightning speed.

While I finished up my drinking,
With caffeine, I started thinking;
How could I use that place setting
To build others up by getting
Deeper in their lives while serving,
Even when they're undeserving;
Since each coffee time goes fast, but,
Used for God, the moments last.

Hurry And Get Up My Friend

The land in which we live today
    is lacking milk and honey -
The world in which we call our home
    is far from peace within;
Just look at all the broken homes
    or shelters without money,
And hear in all the news of crime and sin.

There's death and there's disease abroad
    from drought and malnutrition -
There's violence in our schools and towns
    and wars shown on TV;
If we just sit around and talk
    and not make love our mission,
Then we're just fanning flames, most certainly.

Each one who suffers in this world
    is family by creation -
Each one who cries in anger
    near or far is kinsman, too;
Christ called us all to serve in peace
    the people of each nation,
And share God's love, though some may spit on you.

So hurry and get up my friend
    to serve while you're still breathing -
And hurry to give hope away
    while there's a chance to care;
Don't let this world of hatred keep
    you down with all its seething,
But go and love like Christ to crush despair.

Whether A Day Or Hundred Years

Whether a day or hundred years -
There's trembling at each brink of death;
But with God's grace through blood and tears -
There's no such thing as a dying breath.

The poems in this book were set in 10 point
Century Schoolbook.

OTHER POETRY BY PAUL RAY

If you enjoyed

Flowering Meadows
A BOUQUET OF POETRY

you may also like

Upwords
A FLIGHT OF POETRY
ISBN 978-0-578-03647-2

and

Scattered Glimpses
LEAVES OF POETRY
ISBN 978-0-578-03646-5

and

Open Thoughts
PASSAGES OF POETRY
ISBN 978-0-578-05948-8
available online at lulu.com